SWITZERLAND

MAJOR WORLD NATIONS

SWITZERLAND

James Moore

CHELSEA HOUSE PUBLISHERS
Philadelphia

Chelsea House Publishers

Copyright © 2000 by Chelsea House Publishers,
a division of Main Line Book Co.
All rights reserved.
Printed in Malaysia

First Printing.

1 3 5 7 9 8 6 4 2

Cataloging-in-Publication data available from the Library of Congress.

ISBN 0-7910-5399-7

ACKNOWLEDGEMENTS

The Author and Publishers are grateful to the following organizations and individuals
for permission to reproduce copyright photographs in this book:
J. Allen Cash; Cyma Watch Co., S.A., Douglas Dickens;
Inge Moore; International Photobank; the Swiss National Tourist Office;
Travel Photo International.

CONTENTS

KEY TO PASSES
1 Col de La Forclaz
2 Great St Bernard
3 Simplon
4 Grimsel
5 Brünig
6 Susten
7 Furka
8 St Gotthard
9 Oberalp
10 Lukmanier
11 Mont Cenis
12 Klausen
13 St Bernardino
14 Splügen
15 Maloja
16 Julier
17 Albula
18 Bernina
19 Flüela
20 Ofen
21 Umbrail

GERMAN

FRANCE

FRANCE

R.Rhine

Basel

Aarau

Olten

R.Aare

Solothurn

Central Plateau

Lu

Biel

La Chaux-De-Fonds

Le Locle

Neuchâtel

Murten

BERN

Lake Neuchâtel

Fribourg

Thun

Lake Thun

Lake Br

Bernese Oberland

Aletsch Glac

Lötschberg Railway Tunnel

Si

3

Lausanne

Montreux

Lake Geneva

Rhone Valley

Valais

R.Rhone

Geneva

1

Grande Dixence Dam

Matterhorn

2

Monte Rosa

W.F

GERMANY

Lake Constance

AUSTRIA

Winterthur

R. Limmat

Zurich

Uster

Toggenburg

Lake Zurich

St Gallen

Rhine Valley

LIECHTENSTEIN

Lake Zug

Zug

Lake Walen

Lake Lucerne

Schwyz

Glarus

S

P

⑫

Chur

R. Rhine

Grisons

⑥

⑲

⑨

⑰

St Gotthard Railway Tunnel

⑦

⑧

⑩

Albula
Railway Tunnel

St Moritz

R. Inn

⑳

⑤

⑬

⑭

⑯

⑱

㉑

R. Ticino

Ticino

Piz Bernina

⑮

Tunnel

Locarno

Bellinzona

ITALY

ITALY

⑪

Lugano

SWITZERLAND

Lake Maggiore

Railways

0 5 10 15 20 25 30
KILOMETRES

0   5   10   15
STATUTE MILES

FACTS AT A GLANCE

Land and People

Official Name	Swiss Confederation
Location	Central Europe, east of France and north of Italy
Area	25,806 square miles (41,290 square kilometers)
Climate	Temperate, but varies with altitude
Capital	Bern
Other Cities	Geneva, Zurich, Glarus, Zug
Population	7,260,357
Major Rivers	Rhine, Rhone, Ticino, Inn
Major Lakes	Geneva, Constance, Zurich, Zug, Lucerne, Thun
Mountains	Alps, Jura
Highest Point	Dufourspitze, 4,634 meters
Official Languages	German, French, Italian, Romansch
Ethnic Groups	German, French, Italian, Romansch
Religions	Roman Catholic, 46 percent; Protestant, 40 percent

Literacy Rate	99 percent
Average Life Expectancy	78.88 years

Economy

Natural Resources	Hydropower, timber, salt
Division of Labor Force	Services, 67 percent; manufacturing and construction, 29 percent; agriculture and forestry, 4 percent
Agricultural Products	Grains, fruits, vegetables, livestock, eggs, dairy products
Other Products	Hydroelectricity
Industries	Tourism, machinery, chemicals, watches, textiles, precision instruments
Major Imports	Machinery, chemicals, agricultural products, metals
Major Exports	Machinery, agricultural products, chemicals
Major Trading Partners	European Union, United States, Japan
Currency	Swiss franc

Government

Form of Government	Federal republic
Formal Head of State	President
Voting Rights	All citizens 18 years of age or older

HISTORY AT A GLANCE

2nd century B.C.	The Helvetians, a Celtic tribe, live in the area now known as Switzerland.
58 B.C.**-455** A.D.	The Romans led by Julius Caesar fight the Helvetians and takeover the area as a Roman colony. The Romans open up passes through the Alps that become a link between northern and southern Europe.
3rd century A.D.	Switzerland is invaded by the German-speaking Alemans who settle in the northern plateau.
742-814	Charlemagne conquers each of the cantons in the region and they become part of his Holy Roman Empire.
9th-11th centuries	As part of the Holy Roman Empire the area flourishes. Many abbeys and cathedrals are built as the Church gains more and more control in the country.
12th century	The Holy Roman Empire declines and feudal lords and barons of the region become more powerful. Many disputes between them ensue.
1291	The cantons (regions) of Schwyz, Uri, and Unterwalden form an alliance to defend them-

selves against the feudal rule of the Hapsburgs Austrian Empire. This is the beginning of the Swiss Confederation.

1315	The three cantons defeat the Hapsburgs at the Battle of Morgarten.
14th-early 16th centuries	In succeeding years more cantons join the confederation until there are 13 in 1513.
1476	The Swiss cantons battle against the army of Charles the Bold of Burgundy and establish themselves as courageous and feared soldiers. The Swiss army becomes the greatest fighting force in Europe.
16th century	Calvin and others preach the ideas of Protestantism. This results in religious divisions throughout the country.
1516	The Confederation proclaims its neutrality in European conflicts.
1648	The Swiss Confederation is officially recognized as an independent country after 350 years of rule by the Austrian Empire.
17th-18th centuries	Switzerland sees a period of great prosperity. Banks are established, industry expanded, the arts flourish. Switzerland becomes the most industrialized country in Europe. The highly respected and feared Swiss soldiers are paid to guard most of the royal palaces of Europe.
1789-1803	The French, Austrian, and Russian armies march across Switzerland at various times during the French Revolution and the Napoleonic wars that follow. The country is burned and plundered and the Confederation collapses.

1803	Napoleon establishes a new confederation of 19 cantons.
1848	A federal constitution is agreed upon that creates a central government while allowing each canton to also have its own local government. This constitution is still in effect today.
1914-1918	Switzerland remains neutral in World War I in spite of and because of the ethnic divisions of the country.
1920	With the Declaration of London, the League of Nations recognizes Switzerland's permanent neutrality. It requires that Switzerland participate in any economic sanctions given by the organization.
1939-1945	Switzerland issues a declaration of neutrality in World War II but does prepare its army and citizens for possible invasion. Switzerland becomes a haven for refugees from the war. Later Swiss banks are accused of collaborating with the Nazis.
1950s-1960s	Switzerland makes great strides in industrialization and economic matters. There is very little unemployment.
1971	Women are finally given the right to vote, Switzerland is one of the last countries to do so.
1973	Switzerland and the European Community (EC) agree to the establishment of a duty-free trade area. The agreement helps strengthen the Swiss economy further.
1986	The Swiss vote against membership in the United Nations.
1992	The Swiss reject membership in the European

Union (EU), an economic joining of European nations. The debate divides the country.

1996-1997   Switzerland's dealings during World War II come under international scrutiny with accusations of assisting Nazi Germany monetarily and holding the money of Holocaust victims.

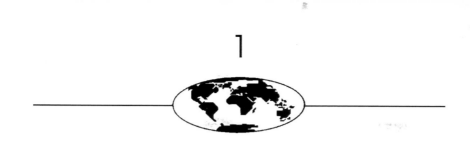

1

At the Crossroads of Europe

Switzerland is one of Europe's smallest countries, both in area and population; yet it is very important commercially. This is largely due to its position at the geographical center of the continent of Europe, astride many of the main routes by which people and goods have, for centuries, moved from one end of Europe to the other.

This small and completely landlocked country is remarkable in another way too—in Switzerland great contrasts exist peacefully side by side. There are contrasts of scenery and, above all, of people with different traditions, cultures, and languages. Nowhere else do people speaking four different languages (German, French, Italian, and Romansh) live in such harmony in so small a space. The Swiss Confederation (as this union of cantons, or states, is called) is a model country.

For all these reasons people from other countries have always been strongly attracted to visit Switzerland for their vacations.

The Julier Pass has been used ever since Roman times. Its majestic scenery is among Switzerland's many tourist attractions.

Every year seven million visitors stream from all parts of the globe to see the glorious countryside and enjoy the famous Swiss hospitality. They are the source of one of Switzerland's largest industries—the tourist industry. But Switzerland is far from being one huge vacation resort. On the contrary, most of Switzerland's wealth comes from manufacturing industry and commerce, in

16

which the country plays a leading role in Europe. There are factories in every corner of the land; and in Swiss towns, banks and business houses are nearly as numerous as cows are on the Alpine meadows.

Like most other European countries, Switzerland has been inhabited from the very earliest times. Remains which have been found in caves high above the level reached by the great glaciers in the last Ice Age prove that Lower Paleolithic and Neolithic man dwelt there. Remains have been found of lake dwellings built 5,000 years ago. One of them, at Geneva, shows the town to be one of the oldest in Europe. Various tribes inhabited the country during the Bronze Age and Iron Age, among them the Celts. One of their settlements (La Tène, on Lake Neuchâtel) revealed such remarkable finds to the archaeologists that they named the Late Iron Age after it.

Of the early inhabitants, the most important tribe were the Helvetii, or Helvetians, who are first recorded in history in the second century B.C. Julius Caesar, who fought them in 58 B.C., when they tried to push into Gaul (now France), described them as one of the best race of fighters he ever met. Today, their name is frequently used to mean "Swiss." CH, the national car registration letters for Switzerland, stands for *Confoederatio Helvetica* (Swiss Confederation). All Swiss postage stamps have *Helvetia* written on them. The chief town of the Helvetians in those ancient days was Aventicum, now Avenches, near Lake Murten. After Caesar's invasion this became a Roman colony as did other parts of the country. Remains of Roman walls or amphitheatres can still be found at Avenches, Brugg, and Augst, all in northwestern Switzerland.

One of the outstanding achievements of the Romans when they expanded their empire was the pioneering of Alpine routes. They opened such passes as the St. Gotthard, Great St. Bernard, Simplon, and San Bernardino. Now that it is easy for us to cross these passes by means of great highways and tunnels, it is strange to imagine with what toil the Roman legions must have clambered along the rocky paths, often knee-deep in snow.

A modern photograph of an old post coach. Even as recently as 100 years ago, horses were the only form of transportation in the Alps.

These routes, once opened, remained a main link between northern and southern Europe. Long trains of pack mules and horses would cross them from late spring till the onset of winter, carrying wares for trading in the markets. Thus the Swiss were given an obvious opportunity to become businessmen and bankers, an opportunity they were not slow to seize. Such towns as Geneva, Bern, Zurich, Basel, and St. Gallen have been trading centers ever since those days.

In the third century A.D., Switzerland was invaded by the Alemans, a German-speaking tribe who settled in the northern plateau. Over the centuries, these people gradually spread throughout the country, except for the west, the corner south of the Alps (now the canton or state of Ticino) and the southeastern corner (now the canton of Grisons). The Aleman settlement is the basic reason for the language differences in modern Switzerland. French is spoken in the west, Italian in Ticino, and Romansh (a language derived from Latin) in a few valleys of Grisons, and German dialects in the rest of Switzerland. The German dialects are known collectively as *Schwyzerdütsch* which means Swiss German. German-speaking Swiss consider *Schwyzerdütsch* to be their national language. It sounds vastly different from *Schriftdeutsch* (written German) which is used for all official purposes and has to be specially taught in the schools. Even if they know German, strangers often find *Schwyzerdütsch* quite impossible to understand.

Going back in history again, we find that in the Middle Ages the country was very much under the control of the Church and

19

Einsiedeln, a famous Benedictine monastery, founded about 934 A.D.

a great many abbeys and monasteries were built. One of the most famous is the Benedictine monastery at Einsiedeln. In those days, what is now Switzerland was not a united country. It consisted of a large number of communities of varying races and languages within the great Holy Roman Empire. As the power of the empire declined, from the 11th century, so the feudal lords and barons became more powerful and many quarrels broke out between them.

The 13th century was the one in which, all over Europe, charters were granted to establish the rights of communities of free men. In England it was Magna Carta, signed in 1215. One of the first parts of Switzerland to receive a charter was the canton of Schwyz, from which the country was eventually to get its name. In 1291, the men of Schwyz made an alliance with the free men of Uri and Unterwalden to defend themselves against their feudal rulers, the Hapsburgs. These three cantons border on the Lake of Lucerne, in the very heart of the country, and are known as the Forest Cantons. Their alliance was the beginning of the Swiss confederation.

The story of William Tell belongs to this period; but, alas, it is

The castle at Sargans, one of the many medieval Swiss fortresses.

no more true than the story of Robin Hood. Tell is only a legendary figure who became a symbol of the Swiss fight for freedom against the Hapsburgs. However, the battle of Morgarten in 1315 in which the Forest Cantons defeated the army of Leopold of Hapsburg is no legend. Fifteen thousand of Leopold's men were utterly routed by 1,500 Swiss who rolled boulders and tree trunks down onto them from the mountains so that they were driven into Lake Aegeri, near Lake Zug.

In the 14th century, first Lucerne (fourth of the Forest Cantons), then Zurich, Glarus, Zug, and Bern joined the confederation while still continuing to rule themselves. In 1386, the Swiss defeated Leopold of Hapsburg in a great slaughter at Sempach. In succeeding years more cantons joined the confederation until, in 1513, there were 13. In the meantime, the Swiss had again shown themselves to be great fighters by beating their last dangerous enemy, Charles the Bold of Burgundy, at Grandson and Murten in 1476. This last war established the reputation of the Swiss as soldiers; for many years afterwards Swiss mercenaries were in demand by every country with a war to fight. Their infantrymen, armed with pikes and halberds, became the great fighting forces of Europe. Even today the pope's bodyguard at the Vatican in Rome is made up of Swiss soldiers who wear a distinctive picturesque costume.

Switzerland played an important part in the Reformation. Zwingli in Zurich and Calvin in Geneva preached the ideas of Protestantism which influenced religious life everywhere During this time, while other countries were fighting long and costly

The pope's bodyguard at the Vatican in Rome, known as the Swiss Guard. Its members are Swiss citizens who wear a picturesque Renaissance uniform.

wars, Switzerland continued to grow, though not without some bloody internal conflicts. Finally, in 1648, the Swiss Confederation was recognized as an independent state.

It was in the 17th and 18th centuries that Switzerland began to develop an international outlook. With Swiss soldiers guarding most of the royal palaces of Europe and even serving as far away as North America, it is not surprising that there was close contact with the outside world. The country became wealthy, banks were established, the arts flourished, and the beautiful countryside began to attract visitors. The government, too, was comparatively wise and fair—and this in an age of despots and dictators.

The French Revolution, and the wars which followed it, put an end to this prosperity. The French, Austrian, and Russian armies marched across the country, burning and plundering. The Swiss

23

naturally resisted, especially when the French tried to impose the French form of government on them. Finally, a new confederation was set up consisting of 22 cantons, all enjoying equal rights. Three of the cantons Unterwalden, Appenzell, and Basel, were divided into two halves to make a total of 25 states. Until 1978, neither the frontiers of the individual cantons nor those of Switzerland as a whole changed, but in that year a new canton was formed. Today, there are 26 cantons. For many years the Roman Catholic, French-speaking inhabitants of the western part of Canton Bern, which is otherwise German-speaking and Protestant, had demanded their own government. Now they have the Canton of Jura, whose capital is Delémont.

Following the setting up of the new confederation, the Swiss people gradually gave their country a uniform national character. It was accepted that the country needed a central government as well as individual cantonal governments. This was achieved by the Constitution of 1848. Since then, Switzerland has had over a century of peace. It was neutral in the two world wars, and has become a very natural location for the headquarters of international organizations, such as the Red Cross and the International Labor Organization as well as the European headquarters of the United Nations Organization.

2

Mountains, Lakes, Rivers, and Forests

Switzerland is Europe's most mountainous country. Apart from the airfields, some lakeside areas, and some wide valleys, there is scarcely a really level spot in the country. Roughly half of the land area consists of high mountains, and another quarter or so consists of lower hills and rolling countryside.

Part of the Swiss Alps, including the famous peaks of Monte Rosa and the Matterhorn.

The Engadine Valley in the Grisons, with its mountains, lakes, and forests, is typical of Swiss scenery.

This makes transportation a special problem. It also has a great effect on where people live; most of them live in the lowlands and valleys. Of a total of some 7,260,357 inhabitants, half live on the Central Plateau, a small area between the two large mountain blocks of the Jura and the Alps. In addition, half the population of Switzerland live in towns or cities with more than 10,000 inhabitants. On the other hand, there are parts of the country, like the high mountain zones of the Engadine and the Bernese Oberland, which are very sparsely populated.

Switzerland is not quite the smallest country in Europe. Both Belgium and Holland are smaller in area; while Denmark is only slightly larger. Unlike these countries, and although so many people live in towns, Switzerland has only one city of more than a million inhabitants—Zurich, which has over 1,100,000. Other large towns are the capital, Bern, Basel, Geneva, the university town of Lausanne, Lucerne, St. Gallen, Winterthur, and Neuchâtel, as well as half a dozen others with over 20,000 inhabitants.

The most obvious features of the Swiss landscape are the mountains. They are really huge and rocky; many of them are snow-capped all year round. The highest peak in the country is Dufourspitze, 15,203 feet (4,634 meters), on the Swiss-Italian border almost, but not quite, the highest in Europe. Nearly everywhere you go in Switzerland you can see these tall mountain ranges with their white caps. On the Central Plateau it is common in clear weather to see the wonderful backcloth of the Alps as you look southeast. The Swiss Alps stretch southwest to northeast. They are a great formidable barrier only pierced by valleys and high passes.

Switzerland has no less than 50 sizeable lakes. This is a view of Lake Constance, the second largest lake in the country.

On the other side of the Central Plateau, to the northwest, are the Jura Mountains, running along the border with France. This range is not spectacularly high but it, too, presents a barrier which is difficult to cross.

Switzerland has no sea frontier, being surrounded by other European countries. To the north is Germany, to the west France, to the east Austria, and to the south Italy. But there are no less than 1,484 lakes, 50 of them quite large. The largest is Lake Geneva, which is big enough to be called an inland sea. Next comes Lake Constance on the German border. Many other "finger lakes," as they are called, lie along the Alpine Foreland. Lakes Zurich, Zug, Lucerne, and Thun are the best known. All these lakes, and many in the Alps, were formed in ancient times by glaciers. Those in the Jura were formed by the folding of the land when the Jura Mountains were thrust up. They were then flooded at a later date. The largest of them are Lakes Neuchâtel, Murten, and Biel.

Water from four of Europe's main rivers gathers in Switzerland. Some drains north into the North Sea through the Rhine River. Some drains south into the Adriatic Sea, through the Ticino River (which flows into the Italian Po River); into the Mediterranean Sea, through the Rhône River; and into the Black Sea through the Inn River, which joins the Danube in Austria. There are many other smaller rivers, too. It is all this moving water which gives Switzerland its most important source of power, hydroelectricity.

At one time, many thousands of years ago, the deep valleys were filled with glaciers. It is possible to see traces of the effect

This valley is typical of large parts of Switzerland, which are covered with dense forest on the lower mountain slopes.

caused by ice which scraped the rocks as it moved forward. There are still over 1,000 glaciers in Switzerland today, though some of them are now very small. The largest is the Aletsch Glacier, which stretches for nearly 15 miles (24 kilometers) and is Europe's largest glacier.

Much of Switzerland is covered with woods and forests, mainly deciduous in the north and the Jura, and coniferous in the rest of the country. About one quarter of the whole land area is densely wooded, thus providing an important source of raw material, timber. About another quarter of the land is considered fit for farming, not counting the Alpine pastures.

Because Switzerland has so many mountains its transportation

The approach to the St. Gotthard Pass. On the left of the picture is an avalanche shelter.

problems are rather special. It is worth having a closer look at the way in which it has tackled them. The Swiss road system is an excellent one. Even very minor roads usually have a made-up surface. In recent years, many stretches of highway have been completed, mostly on the Central Plateau and in the northwest. The most exciting roads are those which run through the mountains. They wind their way by dozens of hairpin bends up to the bare passes, between 5,000 and 6,000 feet (1,640 and 1,968 meters) above sea level, and down again on the other side. In two cases, on the Great St. Bernard and San Bernardino roads, tunnels have been built through the rock some distance below the passes. They can then be kept open all the year round rather than being closed by the heavy snows of winter, as in the past. The most recent major road tunnel is the St. Gotthard Road Tunnel which was opened in September 1980. It is the longest road tunnel in Europe. Now the transport of cars through the rail tunnel, which previously had to be used in winter, is no longer necessary.

Many improvements have been made in mountain roads in recent years by widening the carriageways and smoothing out curves and hairpins. Often this means building enormously expensive tunnels, bridges, and galleries. The Swiss have accepted this as an essential part of running their country. They are very skilled at this sort of engineering. It is often breathtaking to drive along a mountain pass road.

Most of the Swiss mountain roads are served throughout the year by the yellow Alpine motor coaches which are run by the post office. This wonderful bus service is the main transportation between remote mountain towns and villages. The arrival of the post bus is an important event. In the tourist season the bus service is popular with the tourists. They find it an economical way to enjoy a sightseeing holiday in the mountains.

If Swiss roads are an engineering marvel, the railways are often a miracle. The Swiss railway system, one of the world's densest, is probably the best in Europe, perhaps even in the world. The main-line network is run by the state-owned Swiss Federal Railways, founded in 1898. It was the first railway system in the world to be completely electrified. The network covers every part of the country, including many of the remote mountain areas. This has meant great feats of engineering. Many of the 3,250 miles (5,200 kilometers) of line wind their way up remarkably steep slopes. Frequently the trains ascend through spiral tunnels like the one through the Albula pass. (You can watch the engine appear from time to time at a higher level as it labors its way up.) One Swiss railway tunnel, the Simplon, is 12.25 miles (19.5 kilometers) long, the longest in the world. Two others, the St. Gotthard and Lötschberg, are over nine miles (14.5 kilometers) long.

Swiss trains are very modern and clean and keep very good time. The stations, too, are pleasant, well-run places, often with big tubs of flowers on the platforms. Most of them are equipped with excellent restaurants, shops, and waiting rooms. In Switzerland, one of the best and cheapest places to eat is the local railway station restaurant.

The most fascinating of the Swiss railways is the narrow gauge Rhaetian Railway. This operates in the canton of Graubunden (Grisons) in southeastern Switzerland. The train, with its bright red passenger coaches, winds in and out of the valleys, climbing or descending in the most incredible fashion. There are 117 tunnels or galleries and over 480 bridges in the Rhaetian Railway network. A railway enthusiast's dream!

Apart from the conventional railways, there are many other, rather special ones operating throughout Switzerland. There are, for example, the mountain railways used mainly by tourists. Some of them are very unusual. Perhaps the most famous is the Mount Pilatus rack-and-pinion railway which climbs at an angle of 45

The Rhaetian railway crossing the famous Landwasser viaduct before disappearing into a long tunnel.

degrees. Originally it used steam engines, but now it is electric. There are also cable railways, funiculars and lifts in many parts of the country.

Due to very heavy tourist traffic, there is also a good demand

Cable cars like this are an important form of transportation in the Alps.

for water transportation on the many lakes. Over 120 ships make up the fleet of lake steamers.

The most important shipping fleet, though, runs on the Rhine River. This river is Switzerland's largest and most important link with the outside world. There are over 400 Swiss cargo vessels capable of carrying 645,000 tons (655,000 metric tons) of goods on it. Strangely enough, the Swiss also own a fleet of seagoing ships, over 30 of them, in fact, which ply the world's oceans carrying cargo. They also have a major cargo-handling port, at Basel on the Rhine, which deals with over eight million tons (8,128,000 metric tons) of goods per year. These are mainly goods going into Switzerland. There are important plans for the future of Switzerland's waterborne traffic. These include an artificial waterway to link the Rhine and the Rhone, one from Lake Maggiore into Italy, and a third which will make it possible for ships to pass from the upper reaches of the Rhine into Lake Constance.

Air traffic is becoming increasingly important in Switzerland. There are three international airports—at Basel, Geneva and Zurich—used by over 40 different airlines. The Swiss national airline company, called Swissair, is one of the best known in the world. It carries over seven million passengers every year. There are, too, many small charter companies, especially in the mountain regions. These run planes for joy rides, mountain deliveries, and rescue services.

Taking into account its many mountains, Switzerland has one of the world's finest, most efficient and complete transportation systems.

3

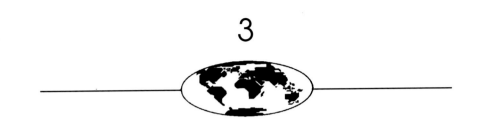

Industry and Commerce

Many people think that most Swiss make a living by running either a hotel or a farm. In fact, this is far from true. Most Swiss have jobs quite unconnected with tourism. Although the tourist industry is one of the most important in Switzerland, the country makes its living by manufacturing a variety of products ranging from foodstuffs to machines and chemicals. These manufacturing industries are vital to the country because they produce goods which can be exported abroad. It is through exports that a country makes the necessary money to maintain its own population.

But Switzerland does not give the impression of being an industrial country. Because of the very poor natural resources there are no heavy industries like mining and steel works which rely on coal and iron ore. Switzerland's industries are all light manufacturing industries which are relatively clean and do not spoil the countryside.

There are no large areas full of factories, as there are in other European countries, with their slag heaps, clouds of smoke, and

Chur, capital of the Grisons, is a typical town in which factories and office blocks blend well into the landscape.

overcrowded towns. Apart from Basel (the Rhine port with its chemical industries), Zurich and Winterthur (both with large engineering works) and St. Gallen (the traditional center of the textile trade) it would be difficult to pinpoint any industrial centers. Perhaps we can say that there are more industries in the north of the Central Plateau than anywhere else, but that is all. Swiss industry is very widely spread throughout the country. Every small town, even village, may have its neat, tidy little factories. None of them puffs black smoke, but they all add their bit to the national output.

How is it that Switzerland has such important industries? After all, it has practically no natural resources only a very little extremely poor coal, timber, limestone for cement, sand and gravel, granite, slate and marble, and clay for bricks. The answer has two parts. First, Swiss industry relies more on skilled labor than on raw materials. Take a watch, for example: highly trained men spend weeks putting it together, but very little raw material is used to make it. This is an ideal situation because the raw material has to be imported at great expense, whereas the skilled labor can be found plentifully in Switzerland. The Swiss people are craftsmen by nature. For centuries, they have been making textiles, pottery, woodcarvings and a hundred and one other things which people

Alarm clocks being assembled at La Chaux-de-Fonds. Switzerland is famous for its clocks and watches.

can make in their homes or in small workshops. Here, too, is a reason why industry is not concentrated in one area.

The second part of the answer is that Switzerland has one raw material which has not been mentioned so far, but which is the most important of all, water power.

Water power is used to generate over 75 percent of Switzerland's electricity and is, therefore, one of the keys to modern Swiss industry. Nearly half of all the electricity generated in Switzerland is used by industry. This is why the factories are so clean and why they need not be centered in any one spot. A glance at the map shows just how many rivers the country has. For the most part, they flow swiftly down the mountain valleys. When water descends rapidly it possesses energy which is wasted unless it is used to turn mill wheels or to generate electricity. There are hundreds of dams as a result of the efforts of Swiss engineers. These dams hold back the water so that it can be released when it is needed to make electricity. Some, like the 935 feet (285 meter) high Grande Dixence Dam in the mountains above the Rhône valley (the highest gravity dam in the world), are truly marvels of engineering. The country is well suited to dam building because of the many narrow river valleys. Swiss dam builders are in great demand in other parts of the world, too, for their advice on how best to build and use artificial lakes.

Other sources of power have to be imported from abroad. The main route for oil and coal is the Rhine River, but there are now pipelines from Italy and France bringing petroleum to refineries in the Rhône Valley and the canton of Neuchâtel.

A view of Switzerland's only port at Basel.

Though a high proportion of everything made by Swiss industries is exported, it is only with the extra income from "invisible exports," such as tourism, insurance and banking, all of which are major industries, that Switzerland earns enough foreign currency to pay for all the imports it needs. And, it needs plenty. Fifty percent of all its requirements have to be imported. In addition to food, virtually all the raw materials used by industry are imported.

The industries which first put Switzerland on the map were textiles and watches, both of them traditional handicraft trades calling for a high degree of skill. Today both these industries have given way in importance to chemicals and engineering.

There was a time when half of all the world's watches were made in Switzerland. At many major sporting events, including the Olympic Games, it is still a Swiss firm which takes the very accurate timings necessary.

There were watchmakers in Geneva in the 16th century, and from there the trade spread to the Jura. Today, the centers of the watchmaking industry are at La Chaux-de-Fonds and Le Locle, both in the Jura Mountains. It is a highly skilled trade, with the major part of its products going to export. Many of the most important inventions in watchmaking, such as self-winding mechanisms, electric, electronic, and quartz watches originated in Switzerland.

Although many of the firms in the watchmaking industry are quite small and do not employ many people, their workshops are extremely modern, light, and airy.

The production of textiles was originally a cottage craft. Even now the Swiss textile industry is quite widespread with many small factories. Most of them are situated in the northeast of the country, around St. Gallen. Silk, rayon, cotton, and all sorts of synthetic fibers are used, but the Swiss are especially known abroad for their light fabrics, embroideries, and furnishing fabrics. Silk ribbons which come mainly from Basel are also world famous, as are the delightful hand embroidered or color printed ladies' handkerchiefs which the Swiss are so good at making.

Le Locle, the center of the watchmaking industry. It is a typical Swiss industrial town with attractive modern factories.

Two other important industries have developed from Switzerland's flourishing and world-famous textile industry. They are chemicals and machine building. In the beginning it was the need for dyes and dressings which encouraged the growth of the chemical industry. Now, concentrated in Basel, where it can get supplies of raw materials easily by way of the Rhine, it produces large quantities of medicines, dyes, insecticides, fungicides, and similar products. Basel is now one of the world's leading centers of chemical production. There are other branches of the industry at Geneva, Bern, and elsewhere.

Originally, the Swiss machine-building industry was involved in making textile machinery, such as weaving looms. Then it received a great boost with the development of hydroelectricity. The industry was soon making turbines, generators, and transformers which gained their manufacturers an international reputation.

All forms of machinery are now made, from diesel engines, cranes, cable railways, and railway rolling stock to machine tools, printing presses, typewriters, calculators, computers, and precision instruments. There are many small and medium-sized firms making very specialized things such as binoculars, movie cameras, and surveying equipment. In fact, anything in which precision is of importance can be found in Switzerland. The machine-building industry has the same tradition for skill as the watchmaking industry.

Swiss industry is very specialized. It does not try to compete where it cannot, such as in the manufacture of automobiles, but concentrates on using the skill of its workers to produce individual goods of high quality. Even in such mass-produced goods as watches there is still a high degree of personal skill required since so much of the assembly is done by hand. By exporting these goods to all parts of the world Switzerland has become what its size and position alone would never have made it, a truly international country.

Before leaving the subject of industry we must mention Swiss food processing, for Switzerland has led the way in this. It was a Swiss, Peter Cailler, who first produced chocolate on a large commercial scale. Nestlé, Suchard, Tobler, and Lindt are other makers

Girls packing boxes of assorted chocolates. Swiss chocolate is world famous for its quality.

of chocolate who are world famous. Malted milk and instant coffee were invented in Switzerland in the last century. Jam, packet soups, all kinds of tinned and packaged foods including cooked meals, tinned and powdered milk, all come from Switzerland with such well-known names as Hero, Maggi, Knorr, and Nestlé. Then there are the famous cheeses, Gruyère and Emmentaler for example, as well as the processed cheeses. Without a doubt, the Swiss food industry is one of the most modern and well-equipped in the world.

What are the rewards for the people behind these achievements? Swiss workers enjoy excellent working conditions. They work a long day, starting at seven o'clock in the morning. But they usually have two breaks, one at nine and one at four, as well as a lunch break. They do little overtime, get well paid and work in modern, healthy conditions which are a model for many other parts of the world. Strikes are very unusual in Switzerland, and there is practically no unemployment.

Besides being famous for their manufacturing industries, the Swiss are, of course, highly regarded as bankers. Ever since the Middle Ages when so much trade passed through the country the Swiss have been important businessmen and bankers in Europe. At one time, they even lent money to the king of France. Today their position is stronger than ever before. The reason for this is

Emmentaler cheeses. They are put on shelves to ripen.

mainly that people in other countries trust the Swiss. They think that Switzerland is a safe country which will have no wars or strikes or changes in government which might upset the economy. The Swiss franc is one of the few currencies in the world which people will accept equally with gold. The advice of Swiss financiers is always sought, and many foreigners invest their money in Switzerland.

In addition to commerce and banking, insurance is an important part of Swiss business life. Success in insurance has been great in recent years in Switzerland, and many Swiss insurance firms do a great deal of international business which brings useful foreign currency into the country.

Canning apricots at a factory at Lenzburg.

4

The Tourist Paradise

Tourism is one of Switzerland's largest and most important industries. At the height of the season as many as 240,000 people are employed in it. Its earnings in foreign currency are as large as those of the chemical industry and larger than those from watches and textiles. The beauty and variety of the scenery, in which Switzerland has no rival, and the charm of the old towns and villages make up one of the country's great natural resources. In fact, a good deal of the land which would otherwise not produce anything is put to very good use by tourism.

Travelers first came to Switzerland in large numbers towards the end of the 18th century as part of what was known as the "Grand Tour." However, it was the Victorians, the British travelers of the 19th century, who really put it on the map as a vacation resort. Men like Edward Whymper, the writer and climber, and travel agents as famous as Thomas Cook and Sir Henry Lunn did much to popularize the Alps. Visitors from other countries quickly followed suit. The Germans, French, Italians, and Dutch were soon making the country their favorite vacation spot. Although there are no figures to prove or disprove it, it is said that Swiss tourism reached its peak before 1914, both in numbers of visitors and in numbers of beds in hotels and guesthouses.

We can certainly show what has happened since records were kept in the 1930s. In 1937, eight million nights were spent in Switzerland by visitors, two million of them by British, with French and Germans coming second and third. By 1978, the position was very different. Then 19 million nights were spent in the country by foreign visitors, with Germany in first place, followed by France, United States, and Belgium, in that order. There was a very large increase in American visitors.

Swiss tourism is a very well-organized industry. Everybody concerned receives a proper training, from the waiter who serves your trout with great skill to the hotel manager who has to make all his guests feel at home. Standards of cleanliness, comfort, and good food are scarcely better in any country. There are over 8,000 hotels and guesthouses in Switzerland and many thousands of private houses, apartments, chalets, and single rooms which could be rented by visitors.

In all, about one million visitors can now be put up at any one time. Of course, they would not all be foreigners for, despite their love of foreign travel, many Swiss people take vacations in their own country.

The Swiss tourist authorities divide the country into 10 regions. These are Grisons (Graubünden), Eastern Switzerland, Zurich and Canton Zurich, Central Switzerland, Northwestern

This highly trained staff in their well-equipped hotel kitchen are typical of the Swiss tourist industry.

Switzerland, Bern and Region, Jura–Neuchâtel–Fribourg, Lake Geneva, Valais, and Ticino.

Graubünden is a mountain paradise, with over 150 valleys dividing its peaks and ranges. It is a region of forest-clad slopes, alpine pastures, and fast-flowing rivers.

Northeast Switzerland, with Lake Constance to the north, has some lofty mountains as well as the foothills of Appenzell. Its highest mountain is the Santis and its deepest lake the Walensee.

Zurich is Switzerland's largest city, a beautiful place astride the

Many people prefer to spend their vacations in chalets such as these rather than in hotels.

Limmat River and fronting on Lake Zurich. Surrounding it are gently undulating stretches of forest, farmland and small lakes.

Central Switzerland has long been a favorite vacation resort. Here is the wildly beautiful Lake of the Four Forest Cantons (Lake Lucerne) and a wide mountain landscape.

Basel, in northwest Switzerland, is an important river port and trading city. Nearby are the steep slopes of the Jura and many medieval castles.

The Swiss federal capital, Bern, is on the doorstep of one of the greatest mountain regions of the country. The Bernese Oberland boasts such famous mountains as the Eiger and Jungfrau. But near Bern is some of the country's finest farmland.

Along the foot of the Jura range are the splendid lakes of Biel, Neuchâtel, and Murten. The wooded slopes of the mountains are clad with chestnut and other deciduous trees, and are planted with vineyards which produce some of Switzerland's best wine.

The city of Geneva, home of the International Red Cross, the European offices of the United Nations agencies and the International Labor Organization, as well as many international businesses, is also the center of a vacation area which stretches down to Montreux. In fine weather from Geneva it is possible to see the snow-clad peaks of the Alps in the misty distance.

The Rhône River rises in the Valais and flows through vine-

Bern, the Swiss capital, is a fine old city which stands in a loop of the Aar River.

yards to Lake Geneva. Not far away are glaciers and craggy mountain peaks, among them the Matterhorn and Monte Rosa.

The Ticino borders on Italy and is very southern in climate and appearance. Its many lakes are a favorite all-year-round vacation resort, while many Swiss go to live on the sunny slopes when they retire from work. The mountains are not very high, but their slopes are steep and covered with trees.

How many other countries can boast of so much scenic beauty in so small an area?

The Swiss tourist year is divided into two seasons, summer and winter. Winter is the longer with approximately 120 days. With the growth in popularity of skiing and other winter sports, it is regarded by many people as the more important season. In fact, many mountain vacation resorts are quite "dead" in the summer as compared with the winter. In the winter there are scarcely enough beds for all those who want to come. Everywhere great efforts are being made to build new hotels and ski lifts.

There is something very special about the Swiss mountains in winter time, when the white slopes ring to shouts of people racing downhill on skis or whizzing round the skating rinks.

By contrast, the summer season has only 90 days. Then, the visitors go to the many lakes as well as the mountains, and the low-land resorts come into their own. They make the most of the short summer (and sometimes spring and autumn as well) for they cannot offer much in the way of entertainment in the winter.

There are many ways in which the visitor to Switzerland can pass his time. Springs and spas with curative powers and high altitude resorts attract those who want to improve their health; one of the most famous is St. Moritz. Then, for those who want to view the countryside there are over 600 mountain railways, many of which are used by skiers in the winter. Over 185 ski schools cater for the learner, but there is ski jumping, skating, curling and ice hockey, too, and the attraction of being able to walk along carefully tended mountain paths.

In summer, climbing is a major sport. Over 39 Swiss peaks exceed 13,500 feet (4,428 meters) in height and there are many smaller ones which make an equally good climb. There are quite a few mountaineering schools, like the one at Pontresina. The mountain huts make it possible for climbers to spend the night in

A splendid view of the Matterhorn from Zermatt.

the mountains, too. Walking is immensely popular, especially with the Swiss, and the whole country is crisscrossed with well marked ways.

Swimming is popular in Switzerland. More and more towns and villages are building heated swimming pools, as are many new hotels. Sailing on the lakes, rowing, canoeing, water skiing, horseriding, golf, and tennis make Switzerland a real sports paradise for all. And we must not forget fishing which, in a country with 20,000 miles (32,000 kilometers) of flowing water, is a very important pastime.

With so many advantages it is hardly surprising that the Swiss tourist industry is one of the most important and largest in Europe.

Right: These climbers are enjoying the exciting challenge of the Swiss Alps.

5

On the Land

Not much more than 100 years ago, most Swiss people earned their living from farming. Now just over four percent work on the land, and the number is steadily falling. But farming is still very important in the Swiss economy because the country has to import 60 percent of all its food which is very expensive. Naturally, the Swiss are keen to produce as much of their own food as they can. So, every plot of land is cultivated and put to good use; in fact, the whole of Switzerland is tended like a garden.

Swiss farms are generally very small. The total area of land suitable for crops and animals is split up between no less than 125,200 farms. The tourist often sees farms which look no bigger than a pocket handkerchief, perched on steep hillsides.

Since modern farming can only be done efficiently with machinery, and normal, large agricultural machines cannot be used properly on small and steep plots, the inventive Swiss have built special small machines, such as grass cutters and mini-trac-

Switzerland is tended like a garden. Most of the farms are very small. These carefully plowed fields are on the Swiss plateau.

tors, which can work on the smallest and steepest hillside. Not many jobs on Swiss farms are done by hand nowadays, and farmers spend a lot of money on equipment that will help them to make their farms pay.

57

One of the things which always surprises foreigners is that there is so much land for farming in Switzerland when the Jura Mountains and the Alps cover such a large part of the country. The reason for this is that mountain pastures alone account for a quarter of all the farming land. The Swiss have adapted their farming to the difficult countryside.

The Swiss grow a great deal of wheat, barley, oats, and maize but still not enough for the country to be self-sufficient. However, they do grow all their potatoes, and some sugar, tobacco, fruit, and vegetables. In addition, most people use their gardens to grow fruit, greens, and vegetables. They are very good at it, even in mountainous areas where the climate can be quite severe. It is quite common to see vegetables occupying the *front* yard of a Swiss house, and in larger towns many people have allotments.

Fruit growing is an important part of Swiss farming. About half of all the fruit trees are apple trees, but there are also pears, plums, cherries, and apricots grown on the Central Plateau and in the Rhône Valley. Much of the fruit is canned or made into jam in factories in the canton of Aargau.

In many parts of the country grapes are grown for making wine. The white wines of the Jura and Lake Geneva are known throughout the world. Red wine, produced mainly in the cantons of Valais and Grisons and along the Rhine, is less well-known. Other regions with large vineyards are Lake Zurich and the canton of Ticino.

But most of the Swiss farms keep cows and specialize in dairy products: milk, butter and cheese. There are two main types of

58

These vineyards on the shores of Lake Geneva are in one of the best-known Swiss wine-producing regions.

Swiss cow, both of which are in great demand in other countries for breeding. This is because they are specially tough and can withstand great differences of temperature. They have to be tough, because the Alpine meadows on which they graze in the summer get very hot on a sunny day and freezing cold at night. This is because they are so high up; sometimes there is even an unexpected fall of snow. The grey-brown cows of Schwyz are the ones shown in most pictures of Switzerland. The other Swiss cows are the red-spotted ones of the Simmental breed. Apart from the meadows high up in the Alps, which cannot be put to any other use anyway, three quarters of all Swiss farming land is used for grazing. A great deal of the milk produced is canned or dried, but much goes into making chocolate and the famous Swiss cheeses for both home and export markets.

Alpine dairy farming is a very special kind of farming. All winter long, the cows live in the valleys. In the oldest type of farmhouse, the cow stalls are on the ground floor, while the farmers and their families live on the first and second floors. The warmth of the cows below helps to keep the houses warm. The cows are fed on hay collected the previous summer. Then, one day in late April or early May, depending on how early the snow clears, the farmers and their cows set out for the high pastures. In fact, practically the whole village joins in, with everyone wearing festive costumes.

This is called the *Alpauftrieb* in German, meaning the driving up of the cows to the "alps," which is the name for mountain pastures. We have the word "transhumance" to describe this moving of livestock from one place to another. Then the cows stay up in the high pastures until the end of the summer, two to three months in all, usually tended by a man, a boy and two dogs. The cowherds live in special timber houses or huts, which may stand alone or be part of a small summer community. The cows all wear bells round their necks. Each bell has a distinctive tone, so that if a cow gets lost it can be tracked down by the noise of its bell. The cows are milked once a day. At one time most of the milk was turned into butter and cheese right there, in the hut, by the cowherd and his helper. They had all the necessary equipment in the hut: churns and pails, moulds and strainers, and shelves on which to store the cheeses until they could be taken down to the valley. It was a fascinating craft and tourists used to climb up to the pastures to watch it going on. Now some milk is sent down to the dairies in the valleys, straight from the cows, in plastic pipelines! This is much cleaner and much more efficient, and it

Schwyz cows in an alpine pasture. All Swiss cows wear bells around their necks so that they may be found if they wander too far.

Late in spring these animals are driven up to the high pastures where they graze during the summer. The villagers who accompany them wear traditional costumes for this festive occasion.

allows the people in the valleys to get fresh cow's milk in the summer. In the old days they used to have to keep goats for milk while the cows were away.

Of course, on a farm the whole family shares the work, including the children. In the mountain cantons the children have very long summer vacations so that they can help with the *Alpauftrieb*, the harvest, and especially the haymaking. In modern Swiss hay-making, the grass is cut by motorized grass cutters or, where the slope is very steep, by hand with a scythe. It is then left on the meadows to dry. During this time it is turned over several times by hand or machine to let the air get to every bit of it, so that it does not rot. When the hay is dry most of it is gathered in bales or simply loaded onto carts and taken down to the haylofts in the valley. The rest is stored in the mountain huts for use the following spring. This activity may go on for several weeks, and often school children from the towns and from youth organizations come up to spend their vacations helping the farmers with this important task.

Today, few of the peasants rely on their farms for their livelihood. Many have a second job as well, usually doing building

A Swiss family haymaking.

work or forestry, helping in hotels, or renting rooms in their houses to tourists. They live a simple life, but their conditions have improved greatly with the increased production of hydroelectricity. Now their houses, though they may be simply furnished, have electric cookers, washing machines, television sets, and all the comforts of modern life. There are very few poor people left in Switzerland today; they all have enough work, even in the mountains.

Such a large part of Switzerland is covered with forest that one might think that Switzerland had enough timber for its own use and for export. But this is not so. Although some of the forest trees are cut down for building timber and for firewood which you can see stacked up in tidy piles against the walls of farm-

Fruit trees and vines in the Bernese Oberland.

Timber from the forests is an important raw material and most towns have timber yards like this.

houses, most of it is left standing to protect farming land. The trees hold back the soil and snow and prevent them from rushing into the valleys in avalanches. They also affect the rainfall over the country, without them there would not be enough water in some areas. As old forests have to be thinned out, new forests are planted all the time.

The Swiss government does quite a lot to help farmers to improve their farming. It loans them money so that they can install plastic milk pipelines, new water supplies, drainage, cable

65

railways, and new farm buildings. The government realizes that, with such a difficult country, special schemes are necessary. It also recognizes, after two world wars, how important it is for such a small, easily isolated country, to be able to produce its own food in a time of emergency.

6

Schools in Switzerland

Switzerland has one of the finest educational systems in the world. The Swiss are born educators. In fact, they can claim to be among the pioneers of modern schooling. For example, Heinrich Pestalozzi (1746-1827), whose theories form the basis for many of the methods used in modern primary schools, was Swiss. There were many others like him who are not so well-known.

Swiss schools are mostly very modern buildings, light and airy, well designed and well equipped for teaching. Of course, there are many older buildings still, especially in remote places. They, too, are extremely well equipped and use very modern methods including many visual aids. In remote areas there are still some one-teacher schools, but then the number of children in the school is always very small. In these cases the authorities try to organize collective classes for older and brighter pupils with other one-teacher schools in the district.

Teaching is a very highly respected profession in Switzerland. The training for teachers is long, usually as long as a complete

Most Swiss schools are bright, modern buildings with good facilities. This school is in Zurich.

university course. But the pay is good, and most teachers stay in the jobs they first take. In any event, transfer from school to school is not easy. In many cantons, teachers are appointed to their jobs for life. In others they are appointed for anything from three to seven years and their re-election may depend on a vote from the parents.

Not only do the Swiss spend more money on schools than any other European country, they also have a large number of libraries in the country and great importance is given to book publishing. Over 4,500 new books are published every year. This is a very high number compared to the population. Swiss books are produced with great care and are a pleasure to look at. Some

68

of the finest printing and publishing in the world is done in Switzerland today.

It is rather difficult to give an overall picture of Swiss schools because the whole system is controlled by the cantons. This means that there are sometimes 25 different ways of organizing things. But the standards of teaching are equally high everywhere, and the certificates students gain are of equal value. This is laid

Schoolchildren enjoying a skiing holiday.

down by federal law, as is compulsory primary education. Nevertheless, the different types of school and different school years are rather confusing.

Each canton controls its own school timetables, teachers, curriculum, and all the business of running the schools, but there are some federal grants. There is, on the other hand, no Ministry of Education or Minister of Education for the country as a whole.

Kindergarten, for children from the ages of four to six or seven, is not compulsory. Nevertheless, many cantons do have such schools. Education proper starts at six or seven and is compulsory for seven, eight, or nine years, depending on the canton. Also compulsory is part-time education for eight hours a week for those who leave school to take up an apprenticeship.

The first school children attend is the primary school; many stay in it until they finally leave school. After three, four, five, or six years, according to the canton, the classes are divided up according to intelligence. Those who do not qualify to enter a secondary or vocational school (that is, a school to learn a trade, such as printing or catering) must enter a full-time nonvocational course which lasts for anything from four months to four years.

Many children leave the primary school or the early grades of the secondary school to take up an apprenticeship. Apprenticeships are very important in the Swiss educational system and last from one to four and a half years according to the trade.

Switzerland has a wide range of training workshops and technical colleges. There are also commercial schools, leading either to a diploma or what is called a Maturity Certificate. Many students stay at secondary school until they are 18, 19, or 20, when they take their Maturity Certificate which is the Swiss Federal requirement for entry to a university. One kind of secondary school is called a *Gymnasium* (German) or, in French-speaking Switzerland, *College, Ecole Superieure* or *Gymnase*. This is the equivalent of the French *Lycée* or English Grammar School.

To see how this system works in practice, let us take a look at three children who want to do very different things.

Hans is extremely clever and wants to be a chemist. After five years in the primary school he goes to a *Pro-Gymnasium* (a kind of preparatory school) for one year, then to a *Gymnasium* until he is 19. He then studies at the Federal Institute of Technology in Zurich for four or five years, at the end of which he qualifies with a university degree.

His sister Heidi, who is not quite so clever, decides to become a top secretary. She leaves primary school when she is 16 to attend a commercial school, full-time, for two or three years, finally qualifying as a secretary capable of getting a very well-paid job.

Their cousin Fritz is good with his hands and is fond of food. He wants to become a baker or pastry cook. So he leaves school at 15 and is apprenticed to the local baker until he is fully trained. He still goes to school for eight hours a week.

Every Swiss boy or girl is very thoroughly trained. Even those who work in shops or workshops do so as apprentices until they have qualified in the job of their choice and can earn a proper wage.

The organization of the school day varies from canton to canton. Even school holidays are very different. For example, summer vacation in the mountain and farming cantons is longer than elsewhere. It lasts from the end of May till the end of August, so that children can help with the harvest and other farm jobs. Most Swiss children get extra school holidays in the winter for skiing, but this is organized by the schools. Teachers take parties of children to skiing centers in the mountains where the schools often maintain buildings especially for this purpose. The children do some schoolwork on this vacation, but the main occupation is skiing. Few children in other countries are so lucky. Again, in the

This craftsman is working in the woodcarving school at Brienz, in the canton of Bern.

summer, schools in the lowlands and towns take parties of children to the mountains for walking, climbing, and outdoor lesson.

Most schools have two free afternoons a week, but children go to school on Saturday mornings. Only a few places have a five-day school week. Strangely enough, it is the teachers who do not want Saturday school abolished. School begins at 7:30 in the morning and finishes about mid-afternoon. Lessons last from 45 to 55 minutes each. Meals are not served at schools, and so children either bring sandwiches or go home for lunch. In many schools, boys and girls are in separate classes, but the trend is towards co-education. The average size of classes is 38 pupils in primary schools, 20 in secondary schools. Parents take a great interest in school affairs. At many schools they have formed a parents' advisory committee which meets regularly with the teachers.

Private schools are extremely numerous in Switzerland. Many are boarding schools which attract foreign pupils. They are in no way controlled by the authorities, but some do follow the same courses as the state schools.

The Swiss university system is very good, but some people think it is wrong that eight cantons, namely those that have universities or colleges at university level, should have to pay for all the university education in the country. There are seven universities: at Basel (the oldest, founded in 1460), Bern, Fribourg, Geneva, Lausanne, Neuchâtel (the youngest, founded in 1909), and Zurich. In addition, there is the Swiss Graduate School of Economics and Public Administration in St. Gallen. The only state-owned universities are the Federal Institutes of Technology in Zurich and Lausanne. Altogether, this is a large number of universities for such a small population. Apart from the Swiss themselves, many foreign students attend them, which shows how highly Swiss education is valued in other countries.

The university at Fribourg. This famous center of learning has very modern architecture.

7

How the Swiss are Governed

One of the most interesting things about Switzerland is its form of government. It is very stable. There are few or no upsets in Swiss politics and there is no danger that the government may suddenly change. It is also the kind of government which makes Switzerland a model democracy. This means that the people have a direct hand in how the country is governed.

The Swiss federal constitution allows the cantons to govern themselves in everything but a few matters. People in the individual cantons have the opportunity to understand what is being done for them and to have a say in it. Moreover, when certain important matters have to be decided upon, a referendum is held in the country in which everybody gets a chance to say "yes" or "no" to the proposal under discussion.

The country is divided into cantons (states or counties). There are 23 main ones, but three of these—Appenzell, Basel and Unterwalden—are again divided into two, giving a total of 26.

Each of these cantons or half cantons has its own government, parliament, and law courts and, in most things, rules itself entirely. It only belongs to the Swiss Confederation by tradition or an ancient alliance. But there is also, of course, a federal or central government for the whole country, which has its seat in Bern, the capital of the country

In five cantons there is still a *Landsgemeinde,* which is the purest form of democracy possible. Here, a public meeting is held annually for people to vote on their cantonal government and to decide important issues. Voting on these occasions is by a show of hands. This form of government remains the same today as it has been for centuries.

The federal government consists of two separate bodies. First, there is the Federal Assembly of 246 men. They choose a Federal Council of seven. These seven men are ministers and are chosen in such a way as to take into account the region they come from, their language, religion, and politics. No two ministers can, at any one time, come from the same canton. In practice, the seven men represent pretty fairly the balance of the country. The seven men together are the head of state and take it in turn each year to be president of the Swiss Republic. The president is really only a kind of chairman and certainly cannot make any decisions by himself.

The Federal Assembly consists of two houses, much on the American pattern. The Lower House is called the National Council and consists of 200 members who are elected every four years by popular vote. It is only since 1971 that women have been

The open-air parliament (*Landsgemeinde*) in Glarus. This form of cantonal government is the oldest in Switzerland.

allowed to vote, Switzerland being one of the last countries to accept female suffrage. Each canton is a constituency with a number of seats in the National Council in proportion to its population. The elections are by proportional representation, which means that the seats are shared out to each party according to the number of votes it gets.

The political parties in Switzerland form eight groups no one of which has ever had an absolute majority, and so the result is a permanent coalition. Since this is not a two-party system, though, there is no actual "opposition," and so there are far fewer quarrels in parliament!

The Upper House is called the Council of States and consists of 46 members, who are chosen by the cantons to represent them. There are two members from each canton, and one each from the half-cantons. Roughly speaking, the makeup of the Council of States (the ancient name for the governing body in the Swiss Confederation) is politically about the same as the National Council.

All federal decisions (that is those concerning the country as a whole) have to be approved by both Houses before they become law.

More important than this is the fact that a referendum is compulsory on any matter which concerns a change in the constitution. All voters in the cantons have an opportunity to decide whether or not to accept a constitutional change proposed by parliament. In addition, all other decrees or acts of parliament may be put to a referendum within three months if 30,000 citizens sign a petition requesting it. This is an extremely fair way of conducting government but it could be very slow if there were many acts

The Federal Palace (*Bundeshaus*) in Bern is the seat of the federal government for all Switzerland.

of parliament in a year. In fact, very few acts of parliament come up to be voted on. Only in a very few cases are they ever rejected. A well-known one was in 1959 when the voters decided against giving the vote to women.

There is another very interesting thing which Swiss voters can do; that is to propose a change in the federal constitution. For this 50,000 signatures are needed. This process is known as the Initiative. The cantonal constitutions provide only for Cantonal Initiatives; that is, proposals to change the cantonal laws. An Initiative is an expensive thing to organize but in recent years there have been as many as two or more a year at the federal level. The government (federal or local) then decides on a course of action. It either adopts the proposal and puts it forward or puts it up for a vote as it stands. Again, no other country in the world has this possibility of asking the government to consider new laws so directly. Experience shows that the Swiss people do not misuse

The Swiss federal government owns the very efficient all-electric mainline network.

the privilege by putting up new ideas all the time and thus making the government's job impossible.

While the cantons are mainly self-governing, the federal or central government is wholly responsible for defense and foreign policy. This is quite natural, since they are things which must be controlled centrally. It also runs a system of social security (pensions, sick benefits, and so on), the railways, the post office, and the telephone service, all of them very efficiently. Incidentally, Switzerland was the first country in Europe to have an STD telephone service and to make it available to all numbers.

80

The remarkable thing about the federal government is that it cannot tell the cantons what to do in local matters. It can only advise them. Of course, it has a budget, but this is smaller than that of all the cantons put together. Out of this budget the federal government gives subsidies to agriculture and for highways, and helps with scientific research. It also runs the Federal Institutes of Technology in Zurich and Lausanne.

Until recently, the Swiss system of government worked very well. There has been a long period of peace and prosperity in the country. But now people are beginning to ask if more central control would not be a good idea. It is thought that there is insufficient cooperation in such matters as roadways and the country's financial situation as a whole. But it is unlikely that the system will change very quickly, because the Swiss people as a whole are very conservative and like to retain without change things which have always worked well.

8

The Swiss People

The Swiss have the highest standard of living of all the nations in continental Europe. This means that salaries and wages are high. People can all afford to dress well, eat well, and live in comfortable houses. There is an almost complete lack of poor people even in the largest cities and the most remote mountain villages. There is electricity in all areas and nearly everybody can afford such things as washing machines, television sets, and telephones.

Of course, it was not always so. Switzerland owes its prosperity and the luxury in which its people live to the way they have adapted themselves to modern industry.

There are four main languages in Switzerland and consequently four types of Swiss people, with the German-speaking ones in the majority. As a whole, Switzerland may be regarded as Germanic. Of course, the people are not entirely separated by their different languages. They mingle freely so that German-speaking Swiss do live in the French-speaking part of the country and vice-versa. Because children at school must learn at least one

A view over the rooftops of Mendrisio in the Italian-speaking canton of Ticino.

other language, as well as their native one, practically all Swiss people speak more than one language fluently. Many speak several, including English which is used widely in business, especially in the tourist trade.

Despite differences of origin and language, the Swiss people are very nationalistic. They are loyal and patriotic to their country. Of course, they are proud of their local dialects and customs, but they think of themselves as Italian *Swiss* or German *Swiss* or French *Swiss*. Since each canton is allowed to run its own government the people from the different cantons never feel inferior to each other. And they never feel that other people are trying to tell them what to do.

There are many foreigners living in Switzerland, too. About 600,000 of these are guest workers in commerce and industry, most of them Italians. In recent years the country's economy has grown so fast that there have not been enough Swiss workers to fill all the jobs. The Swiss government maintains a careful control over the number of foreign workers in the country. Another 280,000 foreigners live in Switzerland. They are people who have chosen to make their home there because they like it so much. These include people from all over the world. Many of them are rich and some are famous.

The Swiss have many qualities which have helped them to make their country wealthy. They are, above all, a very hardworking

The Swiss are very hardworking. They live in comfortable homes and are constantly building new apartments like these.

people. They are efficient too and have many traditional crafts, such as wood carving and weaving. They also save a lot of their money and only spend it carefully. Nearly one-tenth of all the money they earn is saved every year. And they are very shrewd businessmen.

For many hundreds of years, the Swiss have been international-ly-minded. This is because their soldiers and businessmen have found employment in every part of the world. In the last century, large numbers of Swiss emigrated. In the years before 1914, 250,000 Swiss went to the United States alone. On the whole, though, there are no large Swiss colonies abroad except in the countries bordering on Switzerland. This international outlook, has been of great help to the country's modern industries which depend so much on exports.

Despite their modern outlook the Swiss are fond of tradition. They look on all forms of change with suspicion. Some people even regard them as rather stuffy as a result. Not so many years ago there was not a single night club in the country. But this does not mean that the Swiss are a dull people. For example, they dress well, but conservatively; on the other hand, they love to dress up in colorful local costumes. There are many festivals when they can do just this.

Although Switzerland took no part in the two world wars, it still has an important army. This is not a professional army but what is called a militia. This means that all Swiss men are part-time sol-diers. Between the ages of 20 and 50 they have to serve part-time in the army. In their first year, there is four months of basic train-

All Swiss men up to the age of 50 have to serve some time in the army.
This shepherd from Engelberg is enjoying his retirement.

ing. Then before they reach the age of 36, they have to take part in eight three-week training courses. Some further training is given up to the age of 50, and officers have to do even more. Training is hard and often carried out in the mountains. Every man has to take part in shooting practice until he is 40. The crack of rifles can be heard each Sunday from the local ranges all over the country.

People of all kinds come together in the army. University professors mix with laborers and farmers. In every home there is a soldier's uniform and a rifle. Swiss soldiers keep their basic equipment at home; all soldiers can be ready for action at a moment's notice. It is said that Switzerland has more trained soldiers than any other country in western Europe.

As can be imagined, the army plays a very large part in the life of the people. But the country is still very peaceful. Every Swiss citizen believes that his military training ensures a democratic and peaceful way of life.

In spite of its small size Switzerland has had many famous citizens in all walks of life throughout the centuries. Many have become internationally known; and no less than 16 Swiss have been awarded Nobel Prizes.

One of the pioneers of medicine, Paracelsus (his real name was Theophrastus von Hohenheim) came from Einsiedeln and lived from 1492 to 1541. Then there were the members of the great family of the Bernoullis, scientists and mathematicians, in the 17th and 18th centuries. The best-known is Daniel Bernoulli who formulated the theory of the tides. Another famous Swiss mathematician was Leonard Euler (1707-1783) who studied planetary motion. And one of the world's most important philosophers, Jean-Jacques Rousseau (1717-1778), was born and lived in Geneva.

The 19th century saw many more great Swiss names. These included Heinrich Pestalozzi; the historian Jakob Burckhardt; and Carl Jung, the eminent psychologist who worked with Freud. Perhaps the best remembered of all was Henry Dunant who

Some recent designs in Swiss architecture have had worldwide influence. This spendid church is at St. Gallen.

founded the Red Cross in 1864. He was one of the first men to be awarded a Nobel Peace Prize.

In 1979, the Swiss celebrated the centenary of the birth of Albert Einstein, world renowned scientist and originator of the Theory of Relativity, who was a Swiss citizen for many years, though actually born in Germany. For some years he was professor of physics at Zurich University.

In the arts as well as the sciences there are plenty of Swiss names worth mentioning. Modern Swiss painters include Ferdinand Hodler, Paul Klee, and Albert Giacometti. In music there are composers and conductors who are world-famous figures, such as Arthur Honegger and Ernst Bloch (both composers) and the conductor Ernst Ansermet, who died in 1969. Ansermet founded the fine *Orchestre de la Suisse Romande* which ranks with the best anywhere. Another Swiss Nobel Prize winner was the poet Carl Spitteler. His fellow countrymen Gottfried Keller, Max Frisch, and Friedrich Dürrenmatt are among the world's best modern writers.

Perhaps the best known of all great Swiss was the modern architect Le Corbusier. His greatest work is the Indian city of Chandighar, but many buildings and towns have been built to his designs in other parts of the world.

It must be remembered, too, that Switzerland has also been the home of many famous people from other countries. At one time even Lenin lived there. Its peaceful way of life and the beauty of the countryside have made it an ideal place in which to live and work.

9

How the Swiss Live

The Swiss have comfortable homes. Nearly one-fifth of them live in single family houses. But most of the population in the towns live in apartments, many of them in modern apartment blocks. Others live in individual houses divided into apartments. Semi-detached houses are almost unknown in Switzerland, but sometimes rows of houses are built. One-third of all Swiss houses and apartments are owned by the people living in them.

In the country, the villagers and farmers live in houses of traditional design. Each part of the country has its own attractive style of building. Some have wide, overhanging eaves; and wooden balconies all round. Others are built of timber or are clad in wood with paintings or carvings on them.

The Grisons houses are specially fine. They have whitewashed walls with pictures or patterns scratched into the surface. Nearly every house has window boxes gay with flowers in the spring and summer. And it is common to see the national flag, a white cross on a red background, flying from a pole on a balcony or in the garden.

Modern Swiss apartments are seldom without balconies. These are in Zurich.

Inside, the houses and apartments are very comfortable. Most people have central heating, but wood-burning stoves are common in the country, especially in older houses. Great stacks of logs are a common sight outside farmhouses. The living room is usually the dining room as well with a cosy corner for the large table. Kitchens are especially well designed, often with a lot of stainless steel, and there is always a refrigerator. In the bedrooms, the beds usually have large feather-filled duvets on them instead of blankets.

91

Typical houses in the Engadine style, gay with flowers and decorated with patterns scratched into the surface of the walls.

At home, the Swiss people eat simple food. They do not eat a great deal of meat, mainly because it is very expensive. Instead, they have a large number of delicious cheese dishes, such as cheese soups, souffles and the famous *fondue*. Eating *fondue* is a very amusing experience. The cheese is melted in a large pot which stands on the table. Everybody sits round, holding their forks and using them to dip squares of bread into the cheese. This is a speciality of the French-speaking part of Switzerland. Another

92

Swiss speciality—*Rösti*—is also very popular. This is a kind of potato pancake cooked until it is crisp and brown. It is eaten with all kinds of sausages and meat. There are many different types of sausage in Switzerland, almost as many as in Germany

Swiss shops and stores are very well stocked and well run. Even the small villages have attractive, well-filled butchers' and grocers' shops. Nearly all Swiss groceries are now self-service, and there are several important chain stores. Migros deserves a special men-

A simple meal in a Swiss farmhouse.

tion. It is the largest of the large chainstores in Switzerland and it has grown up because its founder wanted to supply food to the ordinary people at the lowest possible price. The organization has over 500 ordinary shops and many traveling shops throughout the country. Besides food shops it also owns petrol stations, factories, hotels, a bank, and an insurance company. Shops in large towns are very well-stocked and extremely modern.

How do the Swiss spend their free time? The answer to this question lies largely in their love of the open air. In summer they spend a lot of time walking or climbing in the mountains. In the winter they nearly all seem to take to skis. Even very small children learn to ski and are just as at home on skis as children in other countries are on bicycles. As keen sportsmen the Swiss excel at ski racing, soccer, and sailing.

The Swiss are great home lovers and spend a lot of time with their families. Reading is a favorite pastime and indoor games like cards are popular. But the Swiss also like to eat in restaurants on the weekends and to visit a café to drink tea and coffee, eat cakes, and talk during their leisure time. In the cities, especially in the north, they show a great interest in concerts and the theater. In the country, many people enjoy singing in choirs and folk dancing.

The Swiss are quite a religious people. The country is almost equally divided between Catholics and Protestants. In most cantons there are some of each. However, Lucerne and the central Swiss cantons are mostly Catholic, as are the Ticino and the Valais. The north and northwest of the country are mainly Protestant.

94

A choir dressed in local costume singing at a festival. Singing and folk-dancing are popular in the country.

In the course of the year there are many festivals in the different regions. But the most important of all is a national one the Swiss National Day, August 1st.

This is a public holiday when everybody goes out in the evening to one of the big entertainments which are organized. There may be fireworks, musical performances, dancing, and

95

In winter, Swiss people of all ages go skiing. These skiers are waiting for the bus to take them to the ski slopes.

long speeches. Lanterns are hung from all the balconies and national flags flown everywhere. Huge bonfires are lit on the hills and on many of the higher peaks. Music festivals are particularly popular in Switzerland. There is one famous music festival held every year in Montreux and another in Gstaad, the latter organized by Yehudi Menuhin, the violinist.

Everywhere in Switzerland the *Schützenfest* is a great occasion. This is a shooting contest. There is a national one as well as all

96

the local and cantonal ones. In some places the shooting is done with medieval crossbows.

Zurich, too, has several festival weeks in June, while Basel has its own very special carnival in February. This is called Fasnacht and is held just before Lent.

In the wine-producing areas there are wine festivals in October, with many people dressed in local costume. In the mountains, there are such things as wrestling contests, horse and cattle-fairs and many traditional local feasts. At all these, the local people dress in their traditional costumes and perform plays and folk dances. There are religious celebrations, too, as on Ascension Day

Alpine horn blowers playing at a folk music evening, Interlaken.

This procession of people wearing strange costumes and funny masks is a traditional part of the Basel Carnival.

when there are processions to the churches. This is particularly true of the Catholic areas of the country.

In all, the Swiss are far from being dull as some people say. In fact, they are a gay and lively folk who enjoy life very much.

GLOSSARY

Alpauftrieb Swiss word for driving cows up to the Alps at the time of harvest

canton State of the Swiss Confederation

coniferous Trees bearing cones such as pine trees that are very common in the forests of Switzerland

ecole superieure Swiss secondary school

fondue A form of eating where you cook the food at the table in a small pot filled with oil or cheese sauce.

funiculars A cable railway ascending a mountain

halberd Weapon used in the 15th and 16th centuries consisting of a battle axe and pike mounted on a six-foot handle

landsgemeinde A pure democracy

rosti Potato pancake

Schriftdeutsch Written German language

Schwyzerdütsch Swiss German language

scythe Tool with a long curved blade at the end of a long handle, used for cutting tall grass

transhumance Act of moving livestock from one place to another

INDEX

Textile industry, 41
Thun, Lake, 28
Ticino, 19, 52, 58
Ticino River, 28
Timber, 64
Tourism, 16, 36, 40, 47, 52, 54
Transportation, 30-35

U

United Nation Organization, 12, 24
Universities, 73-74
Unterwalden, 10, 21, 24, 75
Uri, 10, 21

V

Valais, 51, 58

W

Walensee, Lake, 49

Watch industry, 38, 41
Water power, 39
Wine, 58
Wine festival, 97
Winter sports, 52
Winterthur, 27, 37
Working conditions, 45
World War I, 12, 24
World War II, 12, 13, 24

Z

Zug, 22
Zug, Lake, 28
Zurich (canton), 22
Zurich (town), 19, 27, 37, 49-50, 97
Zurich, Lake, 28, 50, 58
Zwingli, Huldreich, 22